BASIC

CANOEING

TECHNIQUES

by
Rulon Dean Skinner

Photos by Dale H. Olsen

DEDICATION

This book is dedicated to Thane J. Packer!

Now for six years he has been my inspiration while teaching at Brigham Young University. He has inspired me to want to be creative, innovative, and a master teacher.

Without pressure, he has inspired me to achieve a high degree of productivity.

Thane is the epitome of diplomacy.

His style of leadership where he delegates responsibility and along with it full authority to accomplish that responsibility has been appreciated.

When your department chairman can make you feel important, trusted, capable, respected, appreciated, and needed all at the same time, it is near impossible physically to be able to work long and hard enough to justify such confidence. This is the way I have felt for six years now with Thane.

He has demonstrated he cares about my family and its welfare.

His concern about my future is unique. He has worked unceasingly for my university rank advancement—from instructor to assistant professor, and from assistant professor to associate professor. His fairness on salary, teaching load, committee assignment, and student advisement load is appreciated. His continual effort to provide national, regional, and state exposure for me has been with a missionary zeal.

These are only a few of the reasons I dedicate this book to Thane J. Packer as one of the most influential men in my life!

PREFACE

For the past six years that I have taught canoeing on a university level, I have found several good canoeing books, but none with enough pictures to illustrate the various strokes of basic canoeing. This book helps the reader visualize through pictures each canoeing stroke.

The text is intended not only for the university student, but also for anyone new to canoeing interested in learning the basics. It takes the individual without a knowledge of canoeing techniques and teaches him the strokes and skills needed to manage a canoe.

The book is divided into seven sections and each section into topics. Within each topic a step by step approach is used for the stroke or skill.

Designed to be the first of a series of books by different authors which the canoeist would study and use as a reference, this book on basic canoeing techniques should be followed by one dealing with an indepth study of rivers and river canoeing. That one would then be followed by a canoe racing techniques book.

The book may be the text for a university class or it could be used for self-instruction.

Good canoeing!

Rulon Dean Skinner

ACKNOWLEDGEMENTS

To all who contributed to the preparation of this book, I express my sincere appreciation!

Dale H. Olsen served as photographer for the book and took scores of pictures during a university class. From hundreds of pictures, approximately one-third were selected for the book. My appreciation to Dale for his tireless efforts to provide the needed pictures ready for publication.

Jerald K. Jensen, Bruce E. Alger, and Paul Tolman assisted me in demonstrating the various strokes and skills presented. My thanks to them.

Allan R. Whidden completely wrote the section on canoe repair. My sincere appreciation to Allan for sharing his years of experience in canoeing to contribute to the preparation of the book.

Dr. Phyllis Jacobson, Chairman of the Physical Education Department for Women; Dr. Thane J. Packer, Chairman of the Youth Leadership Department; and Dr. Clayne R. Jensen, Dean of the College of Physical Education at Brigham Young University have all supported my efforts to prepare this book. Thanks!

Special acknowledgement is given to my wife, Ruth W. Skinner, who has encouraged me in the preparation.

Rulon Dean Skinner

CONTENTS

BASIC CANOEING TECHNIQUES

Canoeing Basics

Preparation for a Safe Canoeing Experience

Tandem Paddling

Solo Paddling

Advanced Strokes

Preparing for a Canoe Trip

Canoe Repair

CANOEING BASICS

Canoeing Nomenclature

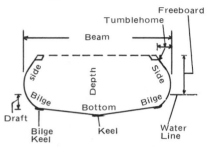

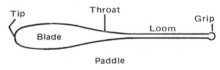

Paddle

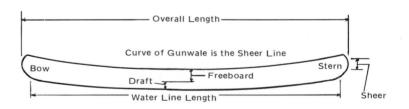

Canoeing Nomenclature

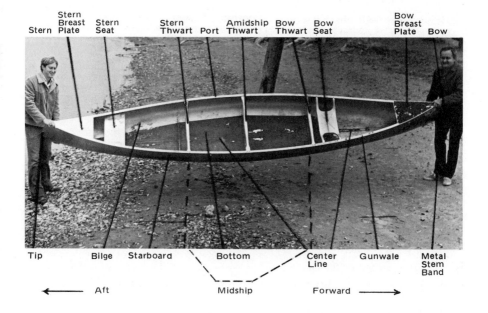

Stern · Stern Breast Plate · Stern Seat · Stern Thwart · Port · Amidship Thwart · Bow Thwart · Bow Seat · Bow Breast Plate · Bow

Tip · Bilge · Starboard · Bottom · Center Line · Gunwale · Metal Stem Band

← Aft · Midship · Forward →

CANOEING LANGUAGE

Abeam—At right angles to the keel line of the canoe.
Afloat—On the water.
Aft—Toward the stern.
Ahead—In front of the canoe.
Amidships—At the center or middle of the canoe.
Astern—Behind the canoe.

Bailing bucket—Any type of container open at one end which can be used to remove water from the canoe.
Beam—Point of greatest width of the canoe.
Bilge—Curved area between side and bottom of canoe.
Blade—The large flat part of the paddle.
Bow—Forward end of the canoe.
Bowman—The person who paddles in the forward position while tandem paddling.
Breast plate—Metal solid piece between gunwales at extreme ends of the canoe.
Broadside—The whole side of a canoe above the water line.

Canoeist—Person who manages a canoe.
Capsize—Turn bottom side up. Upset. Overturn.
Catch—Moment that the paddle comes in contact with the water.
Center Line—Keel line inside the canoe running lengthwise from bow to stern.

Debark—Get out of the canoe.
Deck—Wood pieces fitted between gunwales at the extreme ends of the canoe.
Dock—Platform built on the shore or out from shore.
Double blade—Two-bladed paddle of varying lengths and shapes connected.
Draft—Depth of canoe underwater.

Feather—Flat position of blade during recovery to cut down on water and wind resistance.
Flare—Area of increasing width of the paddle where the loom shaft joins the blade.
Forward—Toward the bow of the canoe.
Freeboard—Portion of the canoe between gunwales and waterline.

Grip—Handle of the paddle.
Grip Hand—Upper hand located on the grip of the paddle.
Gunwale—Upper edge of a canoe's side from bow to stern.

Hull—Body or frame of a canoe.

Keel—Outer strip on bottom of canoe in the center extending from bow to stern.
Keel Line—Center line inside the canoe running lengthwise from bow to stern.
Kneepad—Pad used to support each knee while canoeing.

Landing a canoe—Bringing canoe in to shore, pier, or dock.
Launching a canoe—Putting the canoe afloat.
Leeward—Side or direction away from the wind. (Direction toward which the wind is blowing.)
Loom—Long slender portion of the paddle between the blade and the grip.

Overall length—Distance between bow tip and the stern tip of a canoe.

Paddler—Person who manages a canoe.
Painter—A rope attached to bow or stern.
Pier—Structure extending into the water, used as a walk or landing place.
Pivot—Rotary movement of the canoe with each end moving in the opposite direction.
Planking—Flat sections of wood forming the hull fitted lengthwise next to the canvas.
Port—Left side of the canoe.
Portage yoke—Attachment to canoe used to carry canoe on shoulders. Often the paddles lashed to thwarts form the portage yoke.
Portaging—Act of carrying canoe and gear over land.
Portside—Left side of canoe, facing forward.

Rack—Frame with bars to store or move canoes on.
Rhythm—Action of bowman and sternman paddling in unison.
Ribs—Curved pieces of wood on planking running from gunwale to gunwale.

Shaft—Long slender portion of the paddle between the blade and the grip.
Shaft hand—Lower hand located on the shaft of the paddle.
Sheer—Distance between highest and lowest points vertically on gunwale.
Sheer line—Curve of the gunwale is the sheer line of the canoe.
Slice—Movement of the paddle in the water so that the edge of the blade cuts through the water.
Solo—One paddler alone.
Starboard—Right side of the canoe.
Starboard side—Right side of canoe, facing forward.

Stern—Aft or back end of the canoe.

Sternman—Person who paddles in the rear or aft position.

Stow—Pack. Put away.

Tandem—Two paddlers—one position in the bow and the other in the stern of the canoe.

Throat—Junction of the shaft with blade above the flare.

Thwart—Crosswise braces between gunwales which help canoe maintain its shape.

Tip—End of paddle at blade.

Trim—Canoe balanced evenly on keel by careful positioning of canoeists and equipment.

Wake—Action of the water as a result of canoe movement.

Water line length—Distance from point where water touches bow horizontally to point where water touches stern of canoe.

Windward—Side from which the wind is blowing.

Weight
The canoeist should try several paddles to determine the one that fits him best for weight. A paddle too light will make him work harder than he should. A paddle too heavy will tire him more than normal.

Care
When the paddle is not in use it should be stored out of the sun in a flat position (parallel with the ground) on a supported bottom off the ground. The tip should never be placed on the ground. While handling before boarding the canoe, the paddle should be placed with the tip on the shoe. If the paddler sets it aside, it should be placed in the canoe, set flat on ground or pier, but never leaned with tip or grip on the ground. The loom or shaft near the throat often is protected from water with leather.

Samples of paddles too long and too short for paddlers!

Although paddles are usually made of spruce, other softwood including fir, cedar, and basswood are sometimes used. Hardwood paddles of maple or ash will take the wear and tear from contact with the bottom in shallow water better than softwoods but they are heavier and will warp easier if left lying in the sun.

Paddles

Feel
How the paddle feels to the canoeist is a matter of individual preference.

Length
A good way to measure a paddle for proper length is to stand it vertically in front of you on the tip of your shoe and select one which comes to eye level. A slightly longer paddle is better for the solo paddler because the added length increases leverage.

Grip
Most canoeists prefer the pear-shape grip. Some canoeists prefer the T-shape grip.

Blade
The type of paddle you select depends on the kind of canoeing you do. A good general purpose blade for the beginner is the beavertail blade. The square-tipped blade is used for racing.

Paddles of proper length resting on tips of shoes!

Generally the better grades of single-blade paddles are made of several carefully selected pieces of wood—usually spruce. The grain of the wood is kept flat in the blade and various sections are glued together. In the shaft or loom the grain is placed at right angles to the blade for strength and durability. Paddles manufactured of a single piece of wood are usually heavier.

Canoe trailer for six canoes!

Canoe Racks and Trailers

There are permanent canoe racks usually within a building or shed for the storage of canoes. They should be built with ample space between each rack for easy movement and storage of canoes without touching each other. When storing canoes, place the canoes on the top rack first and move down. Some system should be built to prevent the canoes from slipping from the rack during storage. The reverse sequence is utilized when removing canoes— bottom one first.

Many types of canoe trailers are used to transport canoes from the storage area to the point of use. Above on this page is pictured a six-canoe trailer. Observe the comfortable distance between each canoe. There is no danger here of canoe damaging canoe because of bumps in the road while enroute. Also notice the storage box for paddles, life jackets, and bailing buckets below the bottom canoe. There is a storage box on each side of the rack. Made of sturdy metal, this type of canoe trailer may be purchased commercially or made at home by someone with experience in metals.

In the use of canoe trailers, be sure to have a good method for securing the canoes enroute. On the rack shown above there is a large metal ring welded at the outside end of each metal bar. A similar ring is located on the same bar near the center of the rack. A strong elastic rope stretched between the two metal rings, and snapped onto the outside one will hold the canoe in place while traveling. Also, be sure to have a spare tire for the trailer.

On this page, observe the eight-canoe trailer being used. Note that the trailer has no storage for paddles, life jackets, or bailing buckets and these have to be transported inside the van. Also, because of lack of adequate space between the arms of the rack for the canoes to ride on comfortably while enroute, the van driver has to be constantly alert before starting to move the trailer and while enroute so as to observe that the canoes do not shift positions. A shift from their angled positions could cause damage to the stern and bow undersides.

The four wheel construction for the trailer adds strength and stability. It is important that brake and tail lights on all canoe trailers satisfy state and/or local requirements.

Attention must be given to the trailer hitching system including adequate size ball and hitch as well as safety chain. Maximum standards must be observed in hitching the trailer to the vehicle used in order to protect the canoes as well as people and vehicles traveling behind the canoe trailer.

Car top canoe carrying racks of the one-canoe type may be purchased or rented for the small canoeing group. Each canoe needs to be secured tightly regardless of the type of carrying rack used.

While traveling along highways, attention needs to be given by the canoe trailer driver to be courteous and considerate of other drivers, to use through highways as much as possible, and to keep driving speed moderate. Travel may need to be slowed or curtailed during winds.

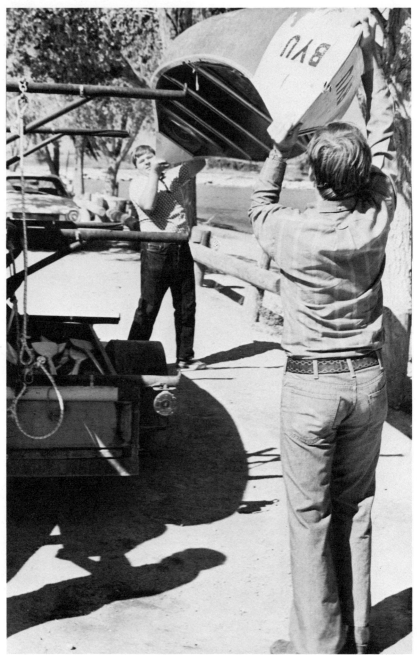

When loading the canoes on the canoe trailer, place a canoe on the top rack first and work down. This allows more working space for the canoeists who have to lift high to reach the top rack. When unloading the canoes from the canoe trailer, the top canoe is the last one to be unloaded. Be very careful to have a firm hold on the canoe when loading or unloading. A dropped canoe will cause permanent damage and may cause leaks to develop.

To unload
Unload a canoe from the trailer rack by unfastening the ropes that hold the canoe secure. Then two persons facing each other move the canoe parallel away from the rack. When the canoe is clear, one person nods or vocally indicates the direction to turn the canoe. It is then carried to the waterway.

To load
The reverse procedure is followed, the canoe being carried to the trailer where it is turned upside down and then fed onto the rack and secured.

Two-man carry to the water. Always carry, never drag!

Carrying a Canoe to Water

Once the canoe is off the trailer or rack, it is carried to the water's edge where it is set down gently to avoid damage. The stern of the canoe is at the water's edge in preparation for tandem paddling.

The canoe is not fed into the water until the canoeists are ready to board.

At the water, canoe is placed stern first on beach.

Preparing the Canoe to Go Afloat

Once at the water's edge with the stern near the water, the canoe is made ready to be put afloat. Involved in this are the following steps:

1) Selection of paddles and putting them inside the canoe.
2) Securing bailing buckets and attaching them to the thwarts.
3) Either wearing the life jackets or placing them in the canoe.
4) Kneepads are either worn or placed in bottom of canoe.

Canoeing Clothing

Clothing for canoeing varies greatly. Dress for comfort, health, and safety. Some hints are given below.

Swimming suits may be worn if weather conditions are conducive—warm enough but not too hot to sunburn. Swimming suits give freedom of body movement, but the canoeist may be pestered by the hot sun or by insects. Usually it will be when canoeing in a confined area such as a camp or section of the lake for short period of time that swimming suits are worn.

Wool clothing such as long johns are considered a must when the weather or water is cold. Wool next to your skin keeps you warm even when wet. You will notice a real difference when you have wool next to your legs which have a tendency to become wet while canoeing. Long trousers rather than shorts are recommended. Wool trousers which are light and loose usually add to the comfort of the paddler. Many canoeists prefer shirts and sweaters which fit snugly.

Shoes are a must. Wearing shoes will prevent many injuries from sharp rocks, sticks, cans, and glass underwater and along the beach. Shoes should be of the type which will allow water out. Wool socks will help keep wet or dry feet warm.

Sweaters or sweat shirts may be added or removed as the temperature changes during canoeing time. A windbreaker is also good.

In order to prevent damage to the eyes, sun glasses are strongly recommended. They should have a band around the head to prevent loss while cruising or when capsizing.

A hat or cap is a must to help keep sunglare from the eyes and the sun off the face. The hat or cap also helps to keep water off your glasses.

A change of dry clothing should be carried with you in a waterproof bag while on a canoeing trip or left in your vehicle during daytime cruising.

Kneepads

Most persons find canoe kneeling position uncomfortable without the use of kneepads. Because the ends of some canoes are slender, one pad will usually do. Those doing lots of canoeing should purchase permanent kneepads or make them. In an emergency the canoeist can make kneepads from almost anything soft including a sweatshirt, sweater, towel, foam rubber, etc.

Keep the following points in mind related to kneepads.
a) They should not soak up water.
b) They should provide some ventilation at the point of contact.
c) They should not slip on the bottom of the canoe.
d) They should be able to float.

Lines

Every canoe should have a painter or line on the bow and on the stern. Sometimes the line attached to the bow is called the bow line and the other the stern line.

These are most valuable for a waterfront area where canoes are kept afloat during the day and stored at night. The painter keeps the canoe attached to the dock or pier while it is not in use. The painter is also handy for towing a canoe.

Each of the two painters should reach to the midship thwart. Stow the lines where they are out of the way while canoeing. Cotton or nylon rope one-quarter inch thick make very good painters.

How to Hold the Paddle

Hold the upper or grip hand comfortably wrapped over the top of the grip so the fingers are away from you. The lower or shaft hand encircles the shaft in the throat area.

Most canoeists prefer a straight lower arm style of paddling. The lower arm should be straight but not tense.

Changing Sides

Tandem paddlers will mutually agree which will paddle on the port side. The other paddler uses the starboard side. The two paddlers should never paddle on the same side. When they are tired of paddling on one side during long trips, or for some other strong reason for changing, one of the paddlers calls out, "Change sides!" and they switch paddling sides. This should not be too frequent.

Bowman's Responsibilities

1) Set the paddling pace or rhythm.
2) Keep an eye out for obstructions under and over the water and warn the sternman immediately when one is spotted.
3) Follow the directions of the sternman.

Sternman's Responsibilities

1) Command the canoe. He is in charge.
2) Call the stroke to be used. Exception is when bowman makes emergency stroke needed to turn canoe out of danger.
3) Steer the canoe.
4) Responsible for safety of all gear.
5) Responsible for safety of all persons in the canoe.
6) Select the landing spot.

Life Jackets or Vests

Life jackets or vests (U.S. Coast Guard—approved type) must be standard equipment for every canoe trip. There must be one for every person in the group.

Life jackets or vests are adjusted to fit each individual before launching a single canoe.

Some states have laws which require an approved life jacket or vest be worn by the canoeist. Others have laws requiring a life jacket for each person be available in the canoe. Canoeists must be familiar with local and state regulations.

A practice session on dry land is a good idea to try before trying the canoes!

Portaging

Portaging is the act of carrying the canoe and all gear from one lake to the next because there is no water connection between them or it is un-navigable.

Portaging is hard work but if time is taken for rests it is within the capabilities of most people. Good physical condition is required for everyone who carries one or more loads weighing from 35 to 100 pounds.

Portages in distance vary in length from a few feet to over a mile.

Step #1
Place the paddles between the amidship thwart which will give a good portage position when canoe is on the shoulders.

Step #2
With the paddles in this position on the thwarts and about a foot apart, lash the paddles to the thwarts using square lashings. This will make a home-made portage yoke.

Note
For canoeists doing a lot of portaging, commercial portage yokes are available.

Step #3
Rest canoe on leg above knee positioning it for flip onto shoulders.

Step #4
Flip the canoe over the head upside down resting the paddles on the shoulders.
Practice distance between paddles to learn best distance for individual comfort.

Step #5
Once upside down on the shoulders, adjust the canoe both sideways and up and down until it is comfortable and balanced. Steady the canoe with the hands on the gunwales. If another man is available, he can lift the canoe tip high while the canoeist carrying the canoe positions himself under the portage yoke. To get the canoe off the shoulders, the procedure is reversed.

Double Blade Paddling

Sometime you might want to try double blade paddling. However, it is not generally used while cruising or racing. It is more of a fun activity to give insight into what kayaking is like.

Double blade paddling may be done while either solo paddling or tandem paddling.

The blades are set or made at right angles to each other. This allows one blade to be feathering while the other is in the water. The hands grip the paddle a little over shoulder width apart. The wrists control the angle of the blade as it enters the water.

The blades are used in a horizontal sweeping action alternately on each side and the canoeist needs to develop an entirely new set of canoeing responses.

Double blade paddling gives more speed once the canoe is moving.

More than this general statement on double blade paddling is not given in this book.

The wisest canoeist develops a deep respect for the weather. An understanding of wind and rough weather as applied to canoeing is essential to prevent capsizing the canoe.

Wind and Rough Weather

The wisest canoeist develops a deep respect for the weather. In case of wind it is best not to be paddling during strong wind. When paddling on a lake, the canoeist must heed the first winds of an approaching storm and head for shore to avoid the dangers caused by the waves. Large exposed bodies of water are to be avoided with any type of threatening weather especially wind. Protected waters found along the windward shorelines of lakes and large rivers may be followed by canoeists during mild winds and rough weather.

If the wind is mild and not the forerunner of a sudden storm, the solo paddler maintains his position near the amidships paddling on the leeward side. He should travel either with the wind or at a diagonal path into it. If these are not possible, then the canoeist will want to shift positions in the canoe so the end from which the wind is blowing has been weighted down. By trial and error, the canoeist determines which side of the canoe is the most effective for paddling. Emergency measures apply in a severe storm and suggest the canoeist get to shore as quickly as possible. Where weather conditions make it impossible to make headway, second best action is to remain in the amidships area and lie down in the bottom along the center line to ride out the storm. Should the canoe capsize in wind and rough weather in addition to the life jacket being worn, the canoe even with water in it can give additional support so stay with it.

When tandem paddlers travel in mild wind and rough weather, they will be wise to add stability to the canoe by each moving toward the amidship for paddling. This allows the ends of the canoe to ride higher over the waves. The sternman should paddle on the leeward side of the canoe. Emergency measures apply in a severe storm and suggest the canoeists should get to shore as quickly as possible. Where weather conditions make it impossible to make headway, second best action is to wait out the storm by sitting or lying down in the canoe. With sizeable waves, keep one end of the canoe into the wind by dragging a paddle over one end as a rudder.

Bail out water that may be taken aboard immediately. It doesn't take much water to seriously affect the stability of the canoe.

If you need to make a landing on the lee shore of a large body of water, be careful the canoe is not whipped or even capsized by the waves as they break and damage is done to the canoe and injury to the canoeist. As you disembark be cautious not to get yourself in a position between the canoe and beach with a large wave headed toward the opposite side of the canoe.

PREPARATION FOR A SAFE CANOEING EXPERIENCE

Swim Checks

Almost all canoeists have capsized their canoes many times. Therefore, it is a must that everyone who uses a canoe know how to swim. Strong swimming ability is required of the canoeist.

Minimum swimming requirements which must be proved before being allowed to use a canoe include the following:

a) Swim at least 100 yards. 75 yards completed with any stroke and 25 yards on the back using an easy resting stroke.

b) Rest by floating as still as you can for a three to five minute period of time.

c) Swim using any stroke at least ten minutes while fully clothed.

The above swimming requirements would be required of everyone using the canoe even those wearing approved life jackets or other life saving devices. Some states have laws which require an approved life jacket be worn by the canoeist. Others have laws requiring a life jacket for each person be available in the canoe. Canoeists must be familiar with local and state regulations.

It is also desirous to require canoeists to prove that they are medically fit for water activities by producing a current [within one year] medical examination completed by a licensed medical doctor.

A person who is a strong swimmer will feel at home in the water and is not likely to panic when the canoe capsizes. He is able to remain calm, to plan, and to execute logical steps for safeguarding or rescuing himself or others.

One of the first practice sessions in canoeing skills must be to demonstrate swimming ability, practice self-rescue techniques, and learn well how to manage the capsized canoe alone and/or with others.

It is important that the canoeist not only have a life jacket or other approved life saving device, but that he wears it. It is also very important that he experience the feel of being in the water with his life jacket on before he has the experience in an emergency.

Overboard

There are a few instruc-
tions when jumping over-
board from a canoe that will
make your jump more effective. The objective of a
proper jump is to enter the
water without going under
and to keep contact with the
canoe at all times.

(a) Stow your paddle so you
won't lose it.
(b) If your jump from the
canoe is intentional to
practice re-entry, remove
your life jacket and stow
it safely in the canoe. [It
is extremely more diffi-
cult while wearing a life
jacket to board a floating
canoe alone.] If your
jump is accidental and
you are wearing a life
jacket, hold it tightly as
you fall or jump so the
pressure of the impact
won't hurt you.
(c) Move to the center of the
canoe, clear of the
thwarts.
(d) Put both hands on the
gunwale on the side you
intend to use for the
jump and your feet to-
gether in the center.
(e) Lean forward, putting
your weight on your
hands and arms.
(f) Lift your legs and vault sideways and overboard. As you go release your
outside hand but maintain your hold on the gunwale with the other
hand. This will minimize the chance of the canoe taking on water.
(g) As you enter the water your legs should be wide apart in a scissor-kick
position to slow your entry. Bring your free arm and hand down flat on
the water slapping it.
(h) Once in the water, maintain your hold on the gunwale and tread water.

Capsized Canoe

If you use proper canoeing techniques your canoe will not capsize and swamp easily in calm water.

When you capsize from a cruising position, you'll find it easy to float or swim out from under the canoe to the surface. The canoe usually floats bottom up.

To right the canoe, pull first on the keel then gently on the far gunwale. If you pull too hard or too fast the canoe will roll.

Once you have righted the canoe look for your paddle, kneepad, and bailing bucket. [This is a good reason why it was important to have tied the bucket to one thwart when you boarded the canoe.] Usually a swamped canoe will not drift away unless it's in a current. Take off some of your heavier clothing and stow it in the bow or stern of the canoe.

Board the swamped canoe near amidships and do it slowly or it will begin rolling. Once in the canoe, you can help maintain balance by extending your arms and legs while sitting on the bottom. Either use your hands or paddle to reach shore, but paddle slowly to maintain your balance in the canoe.

Most swamped canoes of average length will support three people inside. If more than one person is in the canoe, movements should be slow to prevent rolling.

Stay with your capsized canoe and use it as a life raft unless you are on a river and being carried by the current toward dangerous waters such as waterfalls, dams, or other dangerous obstacle. If the water is extremely cold and shore is handy you might want to swim for shore.

The canoe that has been swamped can be righted either on the shore (dock or pier) or by effecting a canoe over canoe rescue.

Climbing Aboard

The challenge while climbing aboard a floating canoe is to do so without capsizing the canoe or allowing it to take on water. The following steps will be helpful.

Step #1 Get back into your canoe about midships where you can grab hold of two thwarts and nothing else will be in your way. If you are wearing a life jacket take it off and put it in the canoe before doing the next step.

Step #2 With both hands on the two thwarts, bring your body to the top of the water using a crawl kick.

Step #3 With a quick arm pull on the two thwarts and a scissor or frog kick, lift and draw yourself forward. The entire process of climbing aboard should be done in one smooth, continuous motion.

Step #4 Reach as far as possible along the thwarts toward the far gunwale pulling your body evenly across the canoe. When your head touches the far side of the canoe execute a quarter turn or roll backward and sit in the canoe.

Method #2 for Climbing Aboard

A second method to use to climb aboard a floating canoe is the following:

Step #1 Get back into your canoe about midships. If you are wearing a life jacket take it off and put it in the canoe before doing the next step.

Step #2 Place your hands on the bottom of the canoe, press down with your hands, and kick your feet to the surface.

Step #3 Your hands should continue to press down, and your feet should kick until the canoe is under your trunk.

Step #4 Keep your head low. When your head touches the far side of the canoe, roll over into a sitting position.

Climbing Aboard

With a quick arm pull on the two thwarts and a scissor or frog kick, lift and draw yourself forward. The entire process of climbing aboard should be done in one smooth, continuous motion.

Reach as far as possible along the thwarts toward the far gunwale pulling your body evenly across the canoe. When your head touches the far side of the canoe execute a quarter turn or roll backward and sit in the canoe.

Canoe Over Canoe Rescue

Step #1
Paddlers giving the assistance come alongside the capsized canoe on the side
away from the canoeist in the water, if possible.

Step #2

Hold capsized canoe and direct canoeists in the water to hold onto your canoe. Transfer equipment in their canoe to yours. Have canoeists in the water move to the far side of your canoe and help balance your canoe.

Canoe Over Canoe Rescue

Step #3

Step #3
Swing the capsized canoe perpendicular to your, then raise it up quickly and turn it bottom up in one motion. Begin to ease the other canoe across the gunwales of your canoe.

Step #4
Feed the other canoe across the gunwales of your canoe until it is balanced and all of the water is out.

Step #5
Roll the capsized canoe over the gunwales of your canoe to an upright position in preparation for setting it back into the water.

Canoe Over Canoe Rescue Step #4

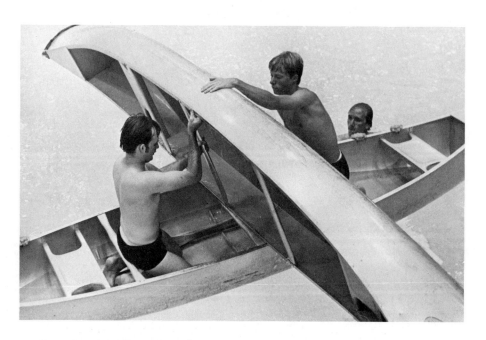

Canoe Over Canoe Rescue Step #5

Canoe Over Canoe Rescue Step #6

Step #6
Ease the other canoe back into the water, feeding it carefully without scraping the gunwales of your canoe.

Step #7
Hold the other canoe by its gunwales alongside yours as the rescued paddlers climb back in and reclaim their equipment. Be careful not to get your fingers between your canoe and theirs.

Swamped Canoe

Canoe over canoe rescue is the best way to empty a canoe which is afloat and has capsized or taken on too much water.

If the canoe becomes swamped near shore, take it to shallow water. After equipment has been moved to shore, one canoeist can stand at either end and pour the water out toward shore or down stream. It then can be turned right side up nearly free of water. Two canoeists working as a team once the water has been poured out, can lift the canoe out of the water and flip it right side up entirely free of water.

If you board (rather than pull with the painter) a capsized canoe, do so near amidships. With your body flat on the water, grab both gunwales and slowly roll over coming into a sitting position on the center line. Once aboard the canoeist(s) must be careful to avoid sudden movements which can start the canoe rolling again as the water shifts from side to side. You should keep your canoe swamped only long enough to safely use one of the methods described to empty it.

Changing Positions While Canoe is Afloat

Method #1

The key factors to remember are to keep your weight centered and low and to use the gunwales for support. Follow the step by step instructions. There are eleven steps.

Step #1
Bowman stows paddle. Sternman holds blade alongside to stabilize the canoe.

Step #2
Bowman moves aft holding onto the gunwales for support and keeping his body in a crouched position.

Step #3
Bowman moves back of the amidship thwart and assumes a crouching position kneeling on the bottom of the canoe and holding onto the thwart in front of himself for support. Keep the elbows near the body.

Step #4
Sternman stows his paddle.

Changing Positions
While Canoe is Afloat

Step #5
Sternman in crouched position with hands on gunwales moves forward.

Step #6
Sternman straddles the bowman as he moves forward.

Step #7
Sternman continues forward
into bow position.

Step #8
Sternman becomes new bow-
man and steadies canoe by
holding blade alongside the
canoe.

Changing Positions
While Canoe is Afloat

Step #9
Ex-bowman continues aft into stern position holding onto both gunwales.

Step #10
Once in position the new sternman takes his paddle.

Step #11
The changing of positions while the canoe is afloat is completed. We now have a new bowman and a new sternman.

Changing Positions
While Canoe is Afloat

Method #2

Key factors to remember
are to keep your weight centered and low and to use the
gunwales for support. Follow
the step by step instructions.
There are ten steps.

Step #1
Bowman stows paddle. Sternman holds blade alongside to
stabilize the canoe.

Step #2
Bowman moves aft holding
onto the gunwales for support and keeping his body in
a crouched position.

Step #3
Bowman moves back toward amidships maintaining his hands on gunwales.

Step #4
Bowman sits on the bottom of the canoe just aft of the amidship thwart.
Sternman stows paddle.

Step #5
Sternman moves past the side of the former bowman holding onto the gunwales as he moves forward.

Step #6
Sternman remains in crouched position with hands on gunwales and walks along keel line of the canoe to the bow position.

Step #7
Ex-sternman takes the bowman position in the canoe and reaches for his paddle.

Step #8
Former bowman prepares to move aft into position. Maintains balance with his hands on gunwales. New bowman holds blade alongside to stabilize the canoe.

Step #9

Former bowman moves into the sternman position maintaining balance with hands on gunwales while new bowman steadies canoe with paddle.

Step #10

The changing of positions while the canoe is afloat is completed. We now have a new bowman and a new sternman utilizing Method #2.

TANDEM PADDLING

Tandem Launching From the Beach

Launch a canoe from the beach when tandem paddling by doing the following steps. [See pictures which illustrate each of the nine steps.]

To launch a canoe from the beach tandem when there is no wind or strong river current is simple and fun.

Step #1

Two canoeists set the canoe down at the water's edge after bringing it from the canoe trailer. The canoe is made ready to launch with the stern entering the water first.

Step #2
Two canoeists pick up the canoe at amidship and lift until it is clear of the ground.

Step #3
Feed the canoe into the water hand over hand until both sets of hands reach the bow.

Tandem Launching From the Beach

Step #4

Bowman steadies bow between knees and with arms crossed over the top of the bow breast plate.

It really doesn't matter for the first launch of the day if the canoe is boarded with the stern in the water first as explained or with the bow first. However, as the canoeists will usually land with the bow toward the beach, most of the time the canoe will be boarded with the stern in the water first and the bow near the beach.

Occasionally both bowman and sternman will need to wade out before boarding in order to have water deep enough to support the canoe without seeing daylight under the keel or scraping it on the bottom. More often the bowman may have to wade out pushing the canoe until it floats free after the sternman is in his position. This is especially important with a rocky beach.

Be sure the lake or river has safe conditions for canoeing before launching in a strong wind. Strong wind usually will cause waves which a canoe cannot handle. Most often it will be wise to wait out the storm. However, if the wind is safe, launch the canoe with the bow first. Place the bow directly into the wind.

Step #5

Sternman moves towards the stern in a crouched position and with hands on the gunwales. He walks along the keel line of the canoe.

Tandem Launching From the Beach

Step #6
When he reaches the sternman's position, the sternman
still crouched low and holding
onto the gunwales makes a
turn 180° in order to be in
proper position facing the
bow of the canoe.

Launch the bow first on a river with a strong current. Angle the canoe on a river with a strong current so the bow is upstream, not in the normal position of being at right angle with the beach.

Step #7
Sternman steadies the canoe with his paddle overside while the bowman releases his hold between his knees and pushes the canoe out onto the water so there will be no daylight under the bow as he boards.

Tandem Launching
From the Beach

Step #8
Bowman boards the canoe facing the bow. He boards in a crouched position and with hands on the gunwales. If the canoe floats free in the water, he pushes off as he boards.

Step #9
Bowman moves aft in the canoe until the canoe's bow lifts free of the shore and the canoe floats on the water. This may happen from the bowman's position or it may not happen until the bowman is amidship. When the canoe floats the bowman moves forward into his regular position and prepares to paddle.

Launching a Canoe Tandem From a Dock or Pier

Launching a canoe from a dock or pier is easier when it's a two-man effort. Follow the steps listed below and you will have no trouble launching the canoe from a dock or pier unless it's extremely windy.

Step #1
Put the paddles, bailing buckets, and kneepads aboard while canoe is on the dock or pier. Two canoeists lift the canoe at amidships until it is clear of the dock or pier.

Launching a Canoe Tandem From a Dock or Pier

Step #2
The two canoeists ease the bow or stern into the water and feed it out hand over hand along the gunwales until it's afloat.

Step #3
Swing the canoe around until it is parallel to the dock or pier. Maintain hold at amidships.

Launching a Canoe Tandem From a Dock or Pier

Step #4

One canoeist holds the canoe while the other boards at amidships with knees bent and holding onto both gunwales. Unless it is windy and the water rough, usually it does not make much difference if the sternman or bowman enters first.

Step #5
The canoeist boarding quickly moves into position in a crouched stance maintaining hands on the gunwales while his partner steadies the canoe from the dock or pier. Canoeist moves along the keel line for balance.

Launching a Canoe Tandem From a Dock or Pier ·

Step #6
Canoeist afloat steadies the canoe with his paddle so his partner can enter.
Much more stability comes from boarding at amidships rather than opposite
the position to be taken.

Step #7

The second canoeist boards at amidships from a kneeling position and reaches for the gunwales as he quickly moves into position from a crouched stance moving along the keel line.

Bow or Forward Stroke

The bow or forward stroke is the basic stroke used to give the canoe forward movement. It is made close and parallel to the canoe with the paddle shaft or loom moving through a nearly vertical plane.

There are four steps to an effective and powerful bow or forward stroke.

Step #1

Step #2

Step #1

Swing the paddle forward to a near-horizontal position. The blade is nearly flat and near the water. The lower or shaft arm is straight. The grip hand is nearly out over the water.

Step #2

As the blade enters the water, the bottom arm pulls directly backward as the upper arm drives forward. This action gives power or forward movement to the canoe. This action continues until the paddle has been pulled back by the shaft or loom hand to the area of the hip. No attempt is made to keep power applied beyond the hip. The power part of the stroke is short. Put your whole strength into this power phase of the stroke.

Step #3

Step #3

Relax both arms and drop the grip hand toward the canoe. This causes the blade to rise above the surface of the water into a position parallel with the water.

Step #4

The blade is kept parallel or "feathered" during the low, wide forward sweep of recovery back to the starting position. Keep the leading edge on the feathered blade slightly elevated during recovery to avoid cutting the water.

Step #4

J Stroke

In tandem paddling the sternman uses the J stroke as needed to keep the canoe on course. The J stroke is a steering stroke used to offset the sideward motion of the canoe resulting from the wind or the strokes of the canoeists. Follow the five steps of the J stroke given on this page and the next few.

Step #1
Begin the J stroke as if you were doing a bow or forward stroke with the paddle forward to a near-horizontal position. The blade is nearly flat and near the water. The lower or shaft arm is straight. The grip hand is nearly out over the water. As the blade enters the water, the bottom arm pulls directly backward as the upper arm drives forward.

Step #2

This action of the bottom arm pulling directly backward as the upper arm drives forward continues until the paddle has been pulled back by the shaft or loom hand to the area of the hip.

J Stroke

Step #3

When the paddle reaches the vicinity of the hip, start turning the blade away from the canoe by turning the thumb in the hand on the grip downward. In the process of turning the blade, exert continual pressure against the water in an outward-backward motion by pushing with the shaft hand and pulling towards you with the grip hand.

In order for the J stroke to be effective, it is important to get the grip hand out over the water to allow the blade to remain as close to the keel as possible and allow the canoeist to lean back and reach as far back as possible.

Step #4
During recovery the blade is "feathered" or parallel to the water. The forward edge of the blade is slightly high to keep from cutting into the water during the recovery.

Step #5
The paddle is returned to the starting or "catch" position to begin another stroke.

Stop

One way to stop a canoe is to stroke in direct opposition to the stroke you were doing. If you were moving forward, both should backwater. If you were doing the draw, do the pushover, etc.

Another way to stop a canoe is for each canoeist to slice the paddle into the water just ahead of their hips with the flat of the blade facing forward. The paddle is then held in a vertical position.

When the canoe is moving fast because of strokes or because of paddling with the current of the river, clamp the shaft or loom of the paddle tightly against the gunwales with the lower hands for an instant stop.

Never hook the thumb on the gunwale. A sprain or dislocation could result.

Hold

Two canoeists can hold their canoe by keeping their paddles in a near vertical position and the blade in the water.

The sternman will steady the canoe by using the hold. With his paddle in the water, he keeps his paddle in a near vertical position. The sternman alone will do the hold during tandem launching and while changing positions afloat.

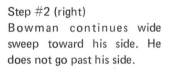

Sweep

From Bowman's Position

Step #1 (above)
Bowman reaches forward toward the bow of his canoe to begin quarter (90°) sweep. The grip hand is held at waist level and the flat portion of the blade faces forward for the sweep. The lower or shaft arm is kept straight during the entire sweep.

Step #2 (right)
Bowman continues wide sweep toward his side. He does not go past his side.

Sweep

From Bowman's Position

Step #3
The blade is kept "feathered "during the recovery to the starting position.
The grip hand remains at waist level. The forward edge of the blade during
the "feathering" or parallel with the water motion is kept slightly high to
prevent cutting the water.

Key points to remember with the sweeps are:

(1) The lower (shaft) arm is kept straight during the entire sweep.

(2) Paddle is held in a near-horizontal position during the entire sweep.

(3) The grip hand is held at waist level.

(4) The flat portion of the blade faces forward for the sweep.

(5) Tandem paddlers use quarter sweeps of $90°$. Solo paddlers use full
sweeps of $180°$.

Sweep

From Sternman's Position

Step #1
Sternman reaches far out to the side with paddle to begin sweeping motion. The grip hand is held at waist level and the flat portion of the blade faces forward for the sweep. The lower or shaft arm is kept straight during the entire sweep.

Step #2
Sternman sweeps toward the stern of the canoe. Pull with the bottom (shaft) hand and push horizontally out with the top (grip) hand.

Sweep

From Sternman's Position

Step #3
Sternman completes the quarter (90°) sweep motion by touching the stern of the canoe with his paddle.

Step #4
Sternman "feathers" paddle back to starting position for next stroke.

Reverse Sweep

From Bowman's Position

Step #1

Bowman reaches far out to the side with paddle to begin sweeping motion toward the bow. The grip hand is held at waist level and the flat portion of the blade faces forward for the reverse sweep. The lower or shaft arm is kept straight during the entire reverse sweep.

Step #2

Bowman sweeps wide toward the bow of the canoe. Push with the bottom (shaft) hand and pull horizontally out with the top (grip) hand.

Step #3 (above)
Bowman completes the quarter (90°) sweep motion by touching the bow of the canoe with his paddle. The grip hand is held at waist level and the lower or shaft arm is kept straight.

Step #4 (right)
Bowman "feathers" paddle back to starting position for next stroke.

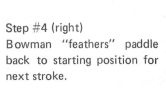

Reverse Sweep

From Sternman's Position

Step #1
Sternman reaches aft toward the stern of his canoe to begin quarter (90°) reverse sweep. The grip hand is held at waist level and the flat portion of the blade is perpendicular to the water. The lower arm is kept straight during the entire reverse sweep.

Step #2
Sternman continues to make a wide sweep toward his side. He does not go past his side. Push with the bottom (shaft) hand and pull horizontally out with the top (grip) hand.

Step #3
Sternman completes the quarter (90°) reverse sweep straight out from his side. He does not go past his side.

Step #4
Sternman "feathers" paddle back to starting position for his next stroke.

Diagonal Draw

A diagonal draw moves the canoe forward as well as sideways.

Step #1
Bowman reaches as far as possible forward and out at approximately 45° angle to begin the diagonal draw.

Step #2
Bowman draws the paddle quickly toward the canoe.

Step #3
As he draws the paddle toward the canoe, the bowman pushes hard on the upper or grip hand and pulls with the lower or shaft hand.

Step #4
Bowman completes the diagonal draw the same way as he completes a bow stroke.

Draw

The draw stroke is used to move the canoe sideways toward the paddling side. It is a powerful control stroke.

Step #1 (left)
Begin the draw stroke by reaching out at a right angle to the canoe The lower (shaft) arm remains straight during the draw stroke.

Step #2 (right)
Push hard on the upper or grip hand. Pull with the lower or shaft hand. Keep your paddle deep. The draw is most effective if you can keep the power on right up to within six inches of the canoe.

Draw

Step #3 (right)
About six inches from the canoe, turn the blade so it can be "sliced" back through the water to starting position. As the blade is turned, the thumb on the grip hand turns up. A quick recovery is important.

When using a lot of force, the canoeist must be careful not to allow the blade to become trapped under the hull as the draw stroke approaches the canoe. If the paddle is swept under the canoe, release your hold on the grip, keeping control with shaft hand.

Step #4 (left)
"Slice" the paddle back through the water to begin another draw stroke. During the draw stroke the blade remains in the water the entire execution of the stroke as well as during recovery.

Pushover

The pushover stroke is used to move the canoe sideways away from the paddling side. It is a control stroke, but less powerful than the draw stroke. Follow the three steps listed to develop an effective pushover stroke.

Step #1

Put the paddle in the water next to the canoe. One way to accomplish this is to "slice" it in from a point straight out from the body. Another way it may be done is to "slice" it in from behind the paddler parallel with the keel.

"Slice" the paddle into the water by entering with the edge of the blade instead of the wide flat part.

Pushover

Step #2
With the paddle in a parallel
position to the canoe, push
with the lower or shaft hand.
Pull with the upper or grip
hand. Keep your paddle deep.
The pushover is much more
difficult to execute than the
draw stroke. The lower
(shaft) arm remains straight
during the entire stroke.

Pushover

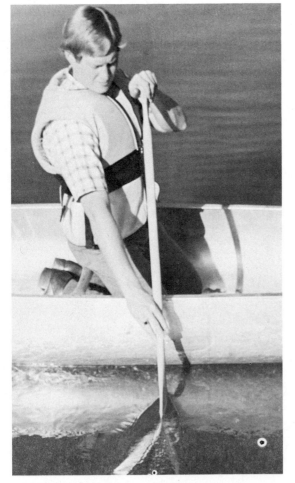

Step #3

When the paddle is approximately two feet away from the canoe, make a quick recovery and begin another pushover. To make a recovery, turn the blade so it can be "sliced" back through the water toward the canoe. As the blade is turned, the thumb on the grip hand turns upward.

When the paddle is next to the canoe in a parallel position repeat the process.

Step #1

Tandem Landing at a Dock or Pier

Step #1
If there is no current or wind, paddle straight toward the dock or pier at a moderate speed. To bring the canoe parallel to the dock or pier, the bowman uses a draw stroke on the side away from the dock or pier and the sternman uses a draw or a sweep. If you end up too far from the dock or pier, the sternman uses the sculling stroke and the bowman the reverse sculling stroke to bring the canoe parallel to the dock or pier.

Step #2
Paddles are stowed in the canoe. Sternman steadies the canoe holding onto the dock or pier.

Step #3
Bowman puts both hands on the gunwales, crouches, and moves aft while still facing the bow. Bowman walks along the keel line to the amidships.

Step #4
Bowman puts one foot and one hand on the dock or pier for balance, then with one shift of his weight steps out.

Step #5
Once out, the bowman holds the canoe while his partner debarks.

Step #6
Sternman puts both hands on the gunwales, crouches, and moves forward along the keel line to the amidship section of the canoe.

Step #7
Maintaining hand contact with the canoe to sustain balance, the sternman steps onto the dock or pier.

Step #2 (left)
Paddles are stowed in the canoe. Sternman steadies the canoe holding onto the dock or pier.

Step #3 (below)
Bowman puts both hands on the gunwales, crouches, and moves aft while still facing the bow. Bowman walks along the keel line to the amidships.

Tandem Landing at a Dock or Pier

Step #4
Bowman puts one foot and one hand on the dock or pier for balance, then with one shift of his weight steps out.

Step #5
Once out, the bowman holds the canoe while his partner debarks.

Step #6
Sternman puts both hands on the gunwales, crouches, and moves forward along the keel line to the amidship section of the canoe.

Step #7
Maintaining hand contact with the canoe to sustain balance, the sternman steps onto the dock or pier.

94

Step #1

Step #2

Removing Canoe from the Water at a Dock or Pier

Step #1 (previous page)
Bring canoe perpendicular with the dock or pier.

Step #2 (previous page)
Each of the tandem paddlers prepare to assist on each side of the canoe in lifting it from the water.

Step #3 (top, this page)
Moving hand over hand along the gunwales, both paddlers pull the canoe from the water being careful the keel does not touch the dock or pier.

Step #4 (bottom, this page)
When the canoe is balanced at amidships between the two canoeists, it is moved to shore and stored.

Tandem Landing at the Beach

Maneuvering a beach landing is easy when you don't have too many obstacles along the shore. On a lake, head straight in. When paddling toward the wind or against a river current, head the canoe toward shore on an angle and at moderate speed. The wind or current will help swing the stern as you slow to a stop.

Land your canoe at the beach when tandem paddling by doing the following six steps. [Pictures demonstrating each step are found on the following pages.]

Step #1
As the canoe approaches shallow water, the bowman carries his paddle, puts both hands on the gunwales, and in crouched position walks his way to the bow and out.

Step #2
The sternman carries his paddle in preparation to debark.

Step #3
Bowman steadies bow between knees and with arms crossed over the top of the bow breast plate to steady the canoe while the sternman debarks. This will also keep the canoe afloat and prevent damage to the keel during landing.

Step #4
With a hand on each gunwale, the sternman in crouched position walks toward the bow of the canoe.

Step #5
Sternman debarks stepping around and balancing himself on the bowman.

Step #6
One canoeist on each side, the tandem paddlers lift their canoe from the water and place it on the shore or store it.

Step #1

As the canoe approaches shallow water, the bowman carries his paddle, puts both hands on the gunwales, and in crouched position walks his way to the bow and out.

Tandem Landing at the Beach

Step #2
The sternman carries his
paddle in preparation to debark.

Step #3

Bowman steadies bow between knees and with arms crossed over the top of the bow breast plate to steady the canoe while the sternman debarks. This will also keep the canoe afloat and prevent damage to the keel during landing.

Tandem Landing at the Beach

Step #4
With a hand on each gunwale,
the sternman in crouched position walks toward the bow of
the canoe.

Step #5
Sternman debarks stepping
around and balancing himself
on the bowman.

Tandem Landing at the Beach

Step #6

One canoeist on each side, the tandem paddlers lift their canoe from the water and place it on the shore or store it.

Tandem Stroke Combinations

PIVOT TURN PORT	**PIVOT TURN STARBOARD**
1) Bowman paddling starboard	1) Bowman paddling starboard
Bowman—Pushover Sternman—Pushover	Bowman—Draw Sternman—Draw
2) Bowman paddling starboard	2) Bowman paddling starboard
Bowman—Sweep Sternman—Reverse Sweep	Bowman—Reverse Sweep Sternman—Sweep
3) Bowman paddling port	3) Bowman paddling port
Bowman—Reverse Sweep Sternman—Sweep	Bowman—Sweep Sternman—Reverse Sweep
4) Bowman paddling port Bowman—Draw Sternman—Draw	4) Bowman paddling port Bowman—Pushover Sternman—Pushover
5) Bowman paddling port	5) Bowman paddling port
Bowman—Backwater Stroke Sternman—Bow Stroke	Bowman—Bow Stroke Sternman—Backwater Stroke

MOVE CANOE BROADSIDE PORT	**MOVE CANOE BROADSIDE STARBOARD**
1) Bowman paddling starboard	1) Bowman paddling starboard
Bowman—Pushover Sternman—Draw	Bowman—Draw Sternman—Pushover
2) Bowman paddling starboard	2) Bowman paddling starboard
Bownan—Reverse Sculling Sternman—Sculling	Bowman—Sculling Sternman—Reverse Sculling
3) Bowman paddling port	3) Bowman paddling port
Bowman—Draw Sternman—Pushover	Bowman—Pushover Sternman—Draw
4) Bowman paddling port	4) Bowman paddling port
Bowman—Sculling Sternman—Reverse Sculling	Bowman—Reverse Sculling Sternman—Sculling

Tandem Stroke Combinations

WIDE TURN PORT

1) Bowman paddling starboard

   Bowman—Bow Stroke
   Sternman—J Stroke

2) Bowman paddlig port

   Bowman—Bow Stroke
   Sternman—Sweep

45° TURN PORT

1) Bowman paddling starboard

   Bowman—Sweep
   Sternman—J Stroke

2) Bowman paddling port

   Bowman—Diagonal Draw
   Sternman—Sweep

STRAIGHT COURSE

1) Bowman paddling starboard

   Bowman—Bow Stroke
   Sternman—J Stroke and Bow
      Stroke as needed. To
      correct for canoe
      veering to the star-
      board, sternman does
      incraased J Strokes To
      correct for canoe veer-
      ing to port, sternman does
      sweeps as needed.

WIDE TURN STARBOARD

1) Bowman paddling starboard

   Bowman—Bow Stroke
   Sternman—Sweep

2) Bowman paddling port

   Bowman—Bow Stroke
   Sternman—J Stroke

45° TURN STARBOARD

1) Bowman paddling starboard

   Bowman—Diagonal Draw
   Sternman—Sweep

2) Bowman paddling port

   Bowman—Sweep
   Sternman—J Stroke

STRAIGHT COURSE

1) Bowman paddling port

   Bowman—Bow Stroke
   Sternman—J Stroke and Bow Stroke
      as needed. To correct for
      canoe veering to the
      starboard, sternman does
      sweeps as needed. To
      correct for canoe veering
      to port, sternman does
      increased J Strokes.

SOLO PADDLING

Launching From the Beach

Step
#2

Launching From the Beach

Launch a canoe from the beach when solo paddling by doing the following ten steps. [See pictures which illustrate each step.]

1) Lift the canoe at amidship, then rest it on the thigh or legs just above the knees as you prepare to feed it into the water.

2) Canoeist reaches the beach thwart with one hand while maintaining balance at the amidship thwart with his other hand as he starts to feed the canoe into the water.

3) Place canoe tip on water and bring hand from amidship thwart to join hand on beachside thwart.

4) Feed canoe into the water moving to the beachside canoe tip while holding the canoe with a firm grip on the breast plate. Position the canoe at right angle to the beach.

5) When the canoe rests on the beach, the canoe tip is up on the beach far enough so the canoe does not blow or float away. Ofttimes while beached, you will be able to see daylight under the keel of the canoe. Never step in the canoe while in this position.

6) The canoe tip is moved near the water's edge before the canoeist boards. It is important that the canoe floats free on the water with no daylight visible under it (as was seen in Step #5 picture).

7) Solo paddler steps into canoe being sure to keep his weight low. He holds onto the gunwale.

8) Firmly holding onto the gunwales of the canoe, the canoeist walks along the keel line of the canoe, maintaining his weight centered and low.

9) Canoeist continues to walk to the solo position for paddling—usually just aft of the amidship.

10) Still balancing himself on the gunwales, the canoeist positions himself with knees in the bilge of the canoe for balance and his buttocks against (not on) thwart.

It really doesn't matter for the first launch of the day if the canoe is boarded with the bow fartherest from the beach. However, as the paddler will usually land with the bow towards the beach, most of the time the canoe will be boarded with the bow near the beach.

The canoeist may have to wade out pushing the canoe until it floats free before boarding. It is especially important that the water is deep enough to support your canoe without seeing daylight under the keel or scraping it on the bottom. This is especially important with a rocky beach.

Step
#3   **Launching From the Beach**

Step
#4

Be sure the waterway is safe before launching a canoe in a strong wind. Strong wind usually will cause waves which a canoe cannot handle. Most often it will be wise to wait out the storm. However, if the wind is safe, launch the canoe with the bow first. Place the bow directly into the wind.

Launch the bow first on a river with a strong current. Angle the canoe on a river with a strong current so the bow is upstream, not in the normal position of being at right angle with the beach.

Step

#5   **Launching From the Beach**

Step #6

Launching From the Beach

Step #7

Step
#8

Launching From the Beach

Step
#9

Launching From the Beach

Step
#10

Launching a Canoe From a Dock or Pier

Usually there will be someone available to help you launch your canoe from a dock or pier. It is certainly easier with two people. However, it can be done alone. Follow the steps listed below.

Step #1
Bend over and grab the two most amidship thwarts. Already have your paddle, kneeling pad, bailing bucket, etc. in the canoe. Note that your knees are bent as you begin to lift the canoe.

Step #2

Pick up and balance the canoe by gradually standing erect while holding the two thwarts. It is important that you do not slide your canoe into the water as you'll scratch it and possibly may damage the keel.

Step #3

Feed either bow or stern tip into the water being careful that the keel at no time touches the dock or pier.

Step #4
Once the canoe is afloat, bring it parallel to the dock or pier.

Step #5
Holding onto both the gunwale and dock or pier, step into the canoe placing the weight of your foot on the keel line.

Step #6
Complete the boarding by keeping your weight low and holding onto the gunwales.

Step #7
In position to solo paddle with the knees in the bilge and the buttocks resting against the thwart (not on it), you are ready to scull away from the dock or pier.

Trim of the Canoe for Solo Paddling

Canoes are sensitive to horizontal and vertical weight distribution and the effects caused by waves, wind, and collisions. The adjustment of fore and aft, up and down, as well as from side to side, plays an important part in canoe handling. A canoe improperly trimmed is hard to handle and is also dangerous. To trim a canoe balance it evenly on the keel by careful positioning of paddler and equipment.

In solo paddling, with calm water and little wind, the canoeist positions himself about a foot behind the exact center of the canoe. This is at the midships thwart if the canoe has the offset center thwart.

When solo paddling against a strong wind, move forward. Paddle on the leewart side of the canoe—opposite the side from which the wind is blowing—and paddle slightly into the wind.

When solo paddling with a very strong stern wind, move back or turn yourself around so the bow is slightly higher than the stern.

When solo paddling in a very strong river current, move back or turn yourself around so the bow is slightly higher than the stern.

When solo paddling with gear aboard on calm water, paddle from the stern thwart with some of the gear stowed toward the bow. This will help trim the canoe.

Remember to trim your canoe according to weight, wind, and water.

Trim of canoe for paddling against a strong wind!

Accented trim of canoe with strong stern wind or very strong river current. Move back or turn yourself around so the bow is *slightly* higher than the stern!

A good trim for calm water and little wind!

The kneeling paddling positions favored by skilled canoeists not only increase stability by lowering the center of gravity but also allow the paddler to use the muscles of his thighs in conjunction with those of his arms more effectively.

While solo paddling the traditional bow and stern parts of a canoe so well defined for tandem paddling may be interchanged to give the best trim. In solo paddling the direction the canoeist faces is called the bow and the part behind him the stern.

Ideal trim of the canoe for solo paddling!

Cruising Position

Kneel on both knees on the bottom of the canoe. Knees should be in the bilge of the canoe, if possible. They should be at least a foot apart. The buttocks should rest on a thwart or the forward part of the seat but not be on top of either. This is the most popular position for recreational or cruising canoeing.

Cruising Relief Position or Single Kneeling position

Kneel on the paddling side. Rest on a thwart or forward part of the seat while kneeling on one knee and extending the other leg forward. Brace the forward foot in some manner.

Proper cruising position!

KNEELING POSITIONS FOR PADDLING

Upright Kneeling Position

Canoeist kneels on both knees, with thighs and trunk erect, and faces slightly toward his paddling side. Keep the knees about 12 inches apart—wider in rough water. This position has several advantages:

a) Allows the canoeist change his location in the canoe irrespective of thwart or seat location.
b) Makes paddling easier if there's a wind.
c) Canoeist can get a more powerful stroke.
d) Good relief from other positions.

Racing Position

The position is essentially on one knee and the opposite foot, with the body erect and facing slightly toward the paddling side. The leg on the kneeling side extends diagonally across the canoe with the bottom surface of the paddler's toes or shoe gripping the bottom of the canoe. The other leg is extended forward with only a slight bend at the knee. Brace the forward foot. This position is used in the organized sport of canoe racing.

What is *wrong* with this upright kneeling position?

J Stroke

The J stroke begins in solo paddling with the blade angled toward the canoe as in the diagonal draw stroke.

Pull the blade toward you while it is angled in a direction toward the canoe as in the diagonal draw stroke.

J Stroke

The J stroke is a steering stroke. It is used almost continuously when solo paddling. It should be executed in such a way as to complement the momentum of the canoe and adjust the direction of the canoe without disturbing the rhythm of the paddler or slowing the forward movement of the canoe.

The J stroke begins in solo paddling with the blade angled toward the canoe as in the diagonal draw stroke. When the paddle reaches the vicinity of your hips, start turning the blade away from the canoe by turning the thumb in the hand on the grip downward. In the process of turning the blade, exert continual pressure against the water in an outward-backward motion by pushing with the shaft hand and pulling toward you with the grip hand.

Most paddlers learning the J stroke have trouble for awhile remembering that when the paddle reaches the vicinity of the hips, turn the blade away from the canoe by turning the thumb in the hand on the grip downward. It is helpful to concentrate during the learning period of this step on the grip hand rather than the shaft hand or the blade itself. Once the turning of the thumb in the hand on the grip downward when the paddle reaches the vicinity of the hips becomes somewhat a habit, the canoeist should focus his attention on leaning back and reaching as far back as possibly as explained below.

Upon completion of the stroke, the blade is in a position with the flat part of the blade parallel to the side of the canoe. Take the blade out of the water. Flatten the blade or relax your wrists to feather the blade so that it is facing the water surface and recover it forward so that a new stroke may be started.

In order for the J stroke to be effective it is important to get the grip hand out over the water to allow the blade to remain as close to the keel as possible and allow the canoeist to lean back and reach as far back as possible.

The inexperienced paddler frequently uses the paddle as a rudder at the end of each stroke. This results in a loss of headway and timing. The J stroke is a smooth, one-count stroke executed with the same rhythm and timing as other strokes. The moment of turning the blade and the degree the blade is turned are determined by the effect needed to keep the canoe on course. Because of the turned blade in the vicinity of the hips, there is a strong tendency for the paddle to cut in toward the canoe as it moves through the water in a straight line to the completion of the stroke. The effective resistance made to overcome this tendency results in forcing the canoe away from the paddling side.

Canoeists differ as to the manner in which the J stroke is done. The stroke is used to control the canoe. The least tiring and most effective interpretation becomes a matter of individual style.

J Stroke

When the paddle reaches the vicinity of the hips, start turning the blade away from the canoe by turning the thumb in the hand on the grip downward. In the process of turning the blade, exert continual pressure against the water in an outward-backward motion by pushing with the shaft hand and pulling towards you with the grip hand.

In order for the J stroke to be effective it is important to get the grip hand out over the water to allow the blade to remain as close to the keel as possible and allow the canoeist to lean back and reach as far back as possible.

Sweep

The sweep is another important stroke to the solo canoeist for steering purposes. The sweep stroke of the solo paddler encompasses an entire side of the canoe of a $180°$ range. The sweep stroke by tandem paddlers has a range of only $90°$.

With the grip hand at waist level and the flat portion of the blade facing forward, extend the paddle toward the bow as far as it is comfortable to reach. Once the blade is about half covered with water, perform a horizontal sweep motion back toward the stern keeping the arm on the paddling side stiff at the elbow and pulling with the shaft or loom hand. In the meantime push horizontally out with the grip hand to employ leverage.

During the sweep, the canoeist should reach as far as possible in the following three directions in order to achieve maximum effect:

(1) forward

(2) sweeping out

(3) aft.

Once the sweep has been made the entire length of the canoe, the shaft or loom hand as well as the grip hand should both be turned forward to place the paddle blade parallel with the water while feathering back toward the bow to begin the next stroke.

The elbow of the arm with the hand on the grip is held near the body and at about waist level while the elbow of the opposite or shaft arm is held stiff during the entire execution of the sweep.

The sweep stroke is used to turn the canoe away from the paddling side.

Sweep

Once the sweep has been made the entire length of the canoe, the shaft or loom hand as well as the grip hand should both be turned forward to place the paddle blade parallel with the water while feathering back toward the bow to begin the next stroke.

Sweep

With the grip hand at waist level and the flat portion of the blade facing forward, extend the paddle toward the bow as far as it is comfortable to reach.

Once the blade is about half covered with water, perform a horizontal sweep motion back towards the stern keeping the arm on the paddling side stiff at the elbow and pulling with the shaft or loom hand. In the meantime push horizontally out with the grip hand to employ leverage.

Reverse Sweep

Occasionally the solo canoeist employes the reverse sweep. It is done in exactly the reverse steps as the sweep. For the solo paddler it encompasses the entire side of the canoe of a 180° range from stern to bow. For the tandem paddlers the reverse sweep has only a range of 90°.

With the grip hand at waist level and the flat portion of the blade facing aft, extend the paddle toward the stern as far as it is comfortable to reach. Place the tip in the water so about half the blade is covered with water. Perform a horizontal sweep motion forward toward the bow maintaining the arm on the paddling side stiff at the elbow and pushing the shaft or loom hand. In the meantime pull horizontally out with the grip hand to employ leverage.

During the reverse sweep, the canoeist should reach as far as possible in the following three directions in order to achieve maximum effect:

(1) aft

(2) sweeping out

(3) forward.

Reverse Sweep
Perform a horizontal sweep motion forward toward the bow maintaining the arm on the paddling side stiff at the elbow and pushing the shaft or loom hand. In the meantime pull horizontally out with the grip hand to employ leverage.

Once the reverse sweep has been made the entire length of the canoe from stern to bow, the shaft or loom hand as well as the grip hand should both be turned clockwise to place the paddle blade parallel with the water while feathering back to begin another stroke.

The elbow of the arm with the hand on the grip is held near the body and at about waist level while the elbow of the opposite or shaft arm is held stiff during the entire execution of the reverse sweep.

The reverse sweep stroke is used to bring the bow of the canoe toward the paddling side.

Inside Pivit

Inside Pivot Method #1

Step #1

Begin the inside pivot by making a wide and full 180° reverse sweep on the paddling side.

The reverse sweep is performed by making a horizontal sweep motion forward toward the bow maintaining the arm on the paddling side stiff at the elbow and pushing the shaft or loom hand. Pull horizontally with grip hand.

Inside Pivot Step #2
At the end of the reverse sweep, turn the paddle so pressure is maintained on one side of the blade.

Step #3
It is important to lean well out so that you can reach far under the canoe while executing a sweep toward the stern. Maintain constant pressure on the same face of the blade during the entire execution of the inside pivot stroke. Continue to maintain pressure as you prepare for another full cycle beginning with a full reverse sweep. The inside pivot is employed when the solo canoeist desires to reverse 180° the direction of the canoe when not moving.

Inside Pivot Method #2

Step #1

Begin the reverse sweep with the grip hand at waist level and the flat portion of the blade facing aft. Extend the paddle toward the stern as far as it is comfortable to reach. Place the tip in the water so about half the blade is covered. Move horizontally out away from the canoe in a circular sweeping motion toward the bow.

Step #2

Half way through the reverse sweep (straight out from the body) completely reverse the paddle by putting the thumb on the grip hand down (toward the body) and elevating the grip arm elbow.

Step #3

With the grip hand and arm in the new position, complete the reverse sweep half of the inside pivot.

Step #4

Lean toward the paddling side as the paddle moves forward.

Step #5
Continue the circular motion under the canoe. By allowing the shaft or loom hand to slide up toward the grip on the shaft or loom, obtain maximum distance under the canoe. The full 360° circle is completed in a horizontal circular sweep.

Step #6
As the inside pivot is completed the grip hand is returned to its original position. The process is repeated the necessary times to complete the 180° pivot of the canoe. It is never done while cruising but always from a stopped position.

Outside Pivot Method #1

The outside pivot gives added impetus to the action of the forward sweep.

Step #1
Begin the outside pivot with a forward sweep. Extend the paddle toward the bow as far as it is comfortable to reach. Once the blade is about half covered with water, perform a horizontal sweep motion back toward the stern keeping the arm on the paddling side stiff at the elbow and pulling with the shaft or loom hand. In the meantime push horizontally out with the grip hand to employ leverage. The solo canoeist does his sweep the full length of the canoe— 180°.

Outside Pivot Method #1

Step #2

As the sweep is completed, swing the paddle over the canoe to the opposite side. The grip goes under your arm and behind you.

Step #3

When the blade is aft and perpendicular to the water, place it in the water. Pressure will come against the front of the blade as you move it forward and the grip will press against your back. Lean back slightly pulling the paddle forward with the shaft or loom hand.

Outside Pivot Method #1

Step #4

As the paddle reaches its forward limits, it will come out of the water and is immediately jumped over the canoe and a new forward sweep begins. The outside pivot is then repeated as needed to completely turn the canoe 180° away from the side the canoeist is paddling on while in a stopped position.

Outside Pivot Method #2

Step #1

Begin the outside pivot with a forward sweep. Extend the paddle toward the bow as far as it is comfortable to reach. Put tip in water.

Step #2

Perform a horizontal sweep motion back toward the stern keeping the arm on the paddling side stiff at the elbow and pulling with the shaft or loom hand. In the meantime push horizontally with grip hand for leverage.

Step #3
The solo canoeist does his sweep the full length of the canoe—180°.

Step #4
After completing the sweep, feather the paddle forward toward and over the tip of the canoe to the opposite side.

Step #5

With the paddle on the opposite side of the canoe, place the grip on the hip pocket. Keep the hand on the grip.

Step #6

With the paddle on the hip pocket, turn the blade of the paddle so it is perpendicular to the water.

Step #7

Once perpendicular, put the paddle in the water and move it forward. The canoeist pulls with the shaft or loom hand and steadies with the grip hand. When the paddle reaches the bow jump it to paddling side.

Step #8

A new sweep begins. The outside pivot is repeated as needed to completely turn the canoe 180° away from the side the canoeist is paddling on while in a stopped position.

Sculling

The sculling stroke moves the canoe toward the paddle. The sculling action is very effective since all movement is positive. Sculling is done with the paddle held in somewhat of a vertical position close to the canoe. The canoeist moves the paddle in a two or three foot path parallel to the keel. The grip hand turns the blade at the beginning of each fore-and-aft movement with the leading edge angle 20° to 45° away from the canoe. When the paddle moves forward, the forward edge of the blade is turned away from the canoe. When the paddle moves aft, it is the aft edge of the blade that is turned away. *Sculling places pressure always on the face of the blade that is next to the canoe.*

The starting action is to apply pressure on the face of the blade next to the canoe while moving the paddle along the two or three foot path parallel to the keel. The smooth rhythm of the sculling stroke is difficult to establish but with a little extra practice it improves quickly.

Reverse Sculling

The reverse sculling stroke moves the canoe away from the paddle. The reverse sculling action is very effective since all movement is positive.

Reverse sculling is done with the paddle held in somewhat of a vertical position only inches away from the canoe. The canoeist moves the paddle in a two or three foot path parallel to the keel. The grip hand turns the blade at the beginning of each fore-and-aft movement with the leading edge angle $20°$ to $45°$ away from the canoe. When the paddle moves forward, the aft edge of the blade is turned away from the canoe. When the paddle moves aft, the forward edge of the blade is turned away. *Reverse sculling places pressure always on the face of the blade that is away from the canoe.*

The starting action is to apply pressure on the face of the blade away from the canoe while moving the paddle along the two or three foot path parallel to the keel. The smooth rhythm of reverse sculling is difficult to establish but with a little extra practice it improves quickly. Much pressure needs to be applied to the shaft or loom hand in order to keep the paddle from striking the canoe.

Backwater

The backwater stroke moves the canoe backwards or stops headway. It begins where the bow stroke stops. The bottom arm pushes forward while the top arm pulls backward. The arm and paddle movements are just the reverse of those used in the bow stroke.

If the canoe is making headway, the backwater stroke is firmly held in the "catch" position until the canoe slows down or stops.

Then hold the paddle in a straight up-and-down position with shaft or loom perpendicular to water. Get the grip hand out over the water when doing stroke. On completion blade faces up.

Stop and Hold

To stop and hold a swiftly moving canoe utilize the backwater stroke then the stop and hold movements.

To stop and hold a slowly moving canoe slice the paddle into the water from the side and hold it in a vertical position with the blade perpendicular to the canoe.

Effectiveness of the hold is increased if the canoeist clamps the paddle tightly against the gunwale with the shaft or loom hand.

Landing a Canoe at the Dock or Pier

Step #1

If there is no current or wind, paddle straight toward the dock or pier at a moderate speed. Use the outside pivot to bring your canoe parallel to the pier and about a foot from it.

Paddles are stowed. If the canoe is to be immediately removed from the water, they are stowed on either side. If canoe is to be tied for additional use, they are stowed on side opposite the dock or pier.

Step #2

Canoeist assumes a crouching position with his feet straddling the keel line and one hand on the gunwale and the other on the dock or pier.

Step #3

Step onto the dock or pier with the nearest foot moving your hand from the far gunwale to the nearest one. Then shift your weight onto that foot, and move the other foot onto the dock or pier. Maintain contact with the canoe with your hands to prevent loss of balance.

Step #4

Bring canoe perpendicular with the dock or pier. Remove canoe from water by moving hand over hand on the thwarts. Be careful the keel does not touch dock or pier.

Step #4

Landing a Canoe at the Dock or Pier

Step #5

Once the canoe is out of the water, balance and carry it to shore. Store on canoe rack.

Equipment should be removed from the canoe immediately. The next person to use the canoe probably will need a different length paddle. Avoid the habit of throwing paddles and equipment onto the dock or pier. This creates hazards for other people and often result in damage to the equipment.

If the canoe is to remain in the water, then after the completion of Step #3 the canoeist would take the painter and secure the canoe to the dock or pier using an appropriate knot for the type of fastening found there.

Landing a Canoe at the Beach

Maneuvering a beach landing is easy when you don't have too many obstacles along the shore. On a lake, head straight in. When paddling toward the wind or against a river current, head the canoe toward shore on an angle and at moderate speed. The wind or current will help swing the stern as you slow to a stop.

Land a canoe at the beach when solo paddling by doing the following steps. [See pictures which illustrate each step.]

Step #1
On a lake, just head the canoe straight in. Approach slowly. "Hold" just before the canoe touches bottom. If you go too fast, the canoe could scrape bottom or even puncture it on some hidden obstacle.

Step #2
Holding firmly onto the gunwales of the canoe, the canoeist walks along the keel line of the canoe, maintaining his weight centered and low in a crouched position.

Step #3
As his hands reach each other at the tip of the canoe, the canoeist balances himself and prepares to step from the canoe.

Step #4
Swinging his rear foot out on the beach, he balances himself. It is important that the canoe not be so high onto the beach that daylight can be seen under the bow. If daylight is seen under the bow, the canoeist may damage the keel as he lands.

Step #5
Immediately he picks up the canoe with one hand holding the breast plate.

Step #6
He walks the canoe completely out of the water being very careful not to drag the keel on the beach. He then removes equipment and stores the canoe.

In wind and on a river the canoe may be freed from the beach by forces other than man if the canoe is not completely removed from the water. This hint may save hours of trying to find lost canoes following a lunch break or overnight stay.

A less common method of landing and unloading is to turn the canoe so that it is parallel to the beach rather than bringing it in bow first. It is unloaded from this position then removed from the water. This method might be more desirable on a rocky beach. Use of this method will get the feet wet.

Landing a Canoe
at the Beach

Step #1
On a lake, just head the canoe straight in. Approach slowly. "Hold" just before the canoe touches bottom. If you go too fast, the canoe could scrape bottom or even puncture it on some hidden obstacle.

Step #2
Holding firmly onto the gunwales of the canoe, the canoeist walks along the keel line of the canoe, maintaining his weight centered and low in a **crouched position.**

Step #3

As his hands reach each other at the tip of the canoe, the canoeist balances himself and prepares to step from the canoe.

Step #4

Swinging his rear foot out on the beach, he balances himself. It is important that the canoe not be so high onto the beach that daylight can be seen under the bow. If daylight is seen under the bow, the canoeist may damage the keel as he lands.

Landing a Canoe
at the Beach

Step #5
Immediately he picks up the
canoe with one hand holding
the breast plate.

Step #6
He walks the canoe com-
pletely out of the water being
very careful not to drag the
keel on the beach. He then removes the equipment and
stores the canoe.

ADVANCED STROKES
(not pictured)

Bow Rudder

The bow rudder moves the bow of the canoe suddenly toward the paddling side. Extend the paddle forward on the paddling side and insert the blade in the water edgewise at an angle of about 20° from the bow. If the blade is inserted too far from the bow, it likely will be caught in the momentum making it impossible to maintain the paddle in the desired position. The 20° angle from the bow is very important.

The shaft hand remains low and slides up so the keel of the hand is braced against the gunwale. The grip hand is braced against the shoulder. The elbow of the grip hand is kept tight against the body.

The bow rudder is used when the canoe has considerable speed because of paddling skill, current, or wind and needs a sudden change of direction without concern for a greatly reduced headway that comes with its application. It may be used to avoid dangerous objects in the river or while landing. The bow rudder is seldom used while cruising.

Cross Bow Rudder

The cross bow rudder moves the bow of the canoe suddenly away from the paddling side. Extend the paddle forward swinging it across the bow and inserting it in the water edgewise at an angle of about 20° from the bow. If the blade is inserted too far from the bow, it will be most difficult to maintain the paddle in the desired position.

The grip hand should be at the side of the body above the hip while the shaft hand is braced in the most comfortable position.

The cross bow rudder is used when the canoe has considerable speed because of paddling skill, current, or wind and needs a sudden change of direction without concern for a greatly reduced headway that comes with its application. It may be used to avoid dangerous objects in the river or while landing. The cross bow rudder is seldom used while cruising.

Stern Rudder

The stern rudder moves the stern of the canoe away from the paddling side. Begin the stern rudder with a reverse (quarter) sweep then maintain the paddle edgewise in the water at an approximate 45° angle to the stern. The grip hand is at waist level and the shaft hand is in regular position.

When used by the beginner, the stern rudder usually is inappropriately used and causes constant reduction of the momentum of the canoe. It should be used only in special situations. It would be used in those special situations when a J stroke could not be used and a course change is desired. One such occasion would be in shallow water. The result of the stern rudder is not evident unless the canoe has moderate to considerable speed.

Cross Draw

The paddle is swung over the bow as would be done in the cross bow rudder. The difference is that the paddle then is not braced, but drawn toward the canoe. The grip hand is held low—down just above the water. Swing the shoulders. It is important the canoeist stay balanced and does not lean out while doing the cross draw.

The cross draw should have only occasional use and should not replace the draw. However, it is effective in shallow water because the blade is horizontal.

Pryaway

The pryaway stroke is done in white water to get the same results as the pushover stroke achieves on flat water. It is done in the water opposite where your knee is on the inside of the canoe (not out from the canoeist's side). Allow the shaft hand to slide up on the shaft. Slice the paddle into the water and under your canoe with the shaft angled away from the canoe. With the blade parallel to the canoe and under it, pry the paddle off the bilge of the canoe. Continue prying until the paddle is beyond vertical position and leaning toward the inside of the canoe.

Feather underwater for the recovery and do another pryaway stroke. The canoeist must maintain extra alertness to his balance with knees firmly in the bilge of the canoe and body balanced over center line or the canoe will capsize.

PREPARING FOR A CANOE TRIP

Preparing for a Canoe Trip

The key to enjoyment and survival on a canoe trip is preparation. Each individual needs to be fully prepared as does the group as a whole. In this section, you will find information that will make your canoe trip more successful.

Lake or River?

Many canoeists will enjoy a canoe trip just for the sake of going on one. Whether they are on smooth or white water is immaterial to them. Others will want the canoe trip for fishing, hunting, or wilderness camping. Again they will feel challenged by smooth water.

When we get into white water canoeing, it usually is for none of the above reasons, rather it is for the sport of conquering turbulent waters which involve the element of risk. If this excites a person, he should join a canoeing club and with others desiring the same experience perfect his river canoeing skills. White water canoeing is not for the beginner nor for the inexperienced canoeist.

Canoe trips normally happen on a large lake or on a river. Sometimes a series of lakes will be connected by water navigable by canoes. Lakes and rivers are rated how difficult they are for cruising.

In the smooth or flat water category, there are three ratings: A, B, and C. All can be handled by the canoeist that understands and has practiced the basic strokes and skills. Rated "A" are pools, lakes, and rivers with velocity under two miles per hour. Rated "B" are rivers with velocity from two to four miles per hour. Rated "C" are rivers with velocity above one mile per hour that have some sharp bends and/or obstructions.

The white water category is more complex being rated from one to six. The canoeist with basic strokes and skills mastered should stay with Rating "1" for his first white water experience. Rating "2" has frequent but unobstructed rapids and the course is usually easy to recognize. Ratings of white water with Ratings "3" or higher should be tried only by the experienced, highly skilled, or expert canoeists. Years of experience are necessary for the ratings above a "2" in the white water category.

Before becoming very involved in river canoeing, the new canoeist will want to secure a river canoeing manual to study and practice with. Also, he will want to seek instruction in river canoeing from an experienced canoeist. One of the good books in this area is Robert E. McNair's *Basic River Canoeing* published by the American Camping Association. (American Camping Association, Inc., Bradford Woods, Martinsville, Indiana 46151)

Instruction as well as opportunities for canoe trips may be found in a number of places including the Explorer program of the Boy Scouts of America (see local Council in your town for details), at universities and colleges, and with private organizations such as Canoeing Clubs, Sierra Clubs, etc.

Canoe Trip Concerns

Canoe trips vary in length and duration. It is best if the beginning canoeist has experience with several one day trips on water before trying the longer ones. This will give him a chance to test his equipment and his skill. A one day trip should probably be no more than ten to twelve miles. Canoe trips provide fun and adventure to both young and adult.

Many things go into the preparation for a canoe trip. You will want to consider the people to go and their abilities to manage a canoe. The size of the group will probably be dictated by the number of canoes available. Tandem paddling is best for canoe trips. Remember there must always be at least two canoes on every trip. Perhaps an ideal number for a canoe trip would be to have a group of six to twelve canoeists.

It is helpful if you can have someone on the canoe trip who is familiar with the area and the water you plan to use.

Qualifications for Canoe Trip Leader

Persons organizing group canoeing trips must meet the minimum requirements for canoe trip leader. As a general rule, it is best to have two leaders because they have 24-hour a day responsibilities. Canoe trip leaders should be at least 21 years of age. The assistant leader should be at least 18 years of age.

Basic qualifications for being the leader of a canoe trip would include the following:

1) Proficiency in canoeing and outdoor skills.
2) Group organizational skills.
3) Maturity of judgement.
4) Enthusiasm for canoeing trips.
5) Pleasant personality.
6) First Aid training. (The American National Red Cross Standard First Aid and Personal Safety course would be excellent preparation in first aid.)

Basic Considerations

There are many considerations for canoe trips. Some of the basic are:

1) Who should go?
2) Where should the trip be?
3) How long should the trip last?
4) When should the trip depart?
5) What specific prerequisites should be met before the trip?

Trip Schedule

Included in the canoe trip schedule should be:

1) The route.
2) Each day's schedule.
3) Identification of the site for each day's stop.

Copies of the trip schedule should be filed before leaving home with families of those participating and with appropriate governmental agencies (Park Ranger, County Sheriff, etc.) of the area where the trip is to happen. You never know when someone will need to find your group because of an emergency back home. Also, it's good insurance that help will know where to look should you have problems and fail to return on schedule.

Pre-trip Orientation

Before every canoeing trip there should be one or more pre-trip orientation meetings or sessions. During this time routes are studied, landmarks to be seen enroute identified, areas of specific interest reviewed, in-camp activities finalized, menu developed, cooking methods tested, canoes and related equipment field tested and any needed repairs made, camping equipment tested, and trip courtesy and manners reviewed.

A proper pre-trip orientation often makes the difference between just a trip and an outstanding, fulfilling experience. Another key to a successful canoeing trip is to have every member of the group with definite group duties.

Etiquette for Canoe Trips

Good personal conduct makes a difference not only to your group but to other groups canoeing or camping near you. Although the golden rule would cover all the etiquette needed for canoe trips, below find specifics as applied to canoeing:

1) Be considerate of other canoeists and campers. On the water as you meet them, be courteous. Avoid banging canoes, shouting, etc.— especially during the night and early morning. Be considerate within your own group.

2) Related to sanitation during a canoe trip, stay away of lakes and rivers at least 100 feet. Try to be clean as a cat. Individual "cat hole" should be dug deep in an appropriate place, used, and then covered. Respect the privacy of the opposite sex.

3) Carry out anything you don't use that you brought along. This includes empty cans, paper, etc. It is important to have individual litter bags. Don't pollute the waterways. Leave your campsite clean.

4) Be sure to do your share of the paddling.

5) Take care of your canoe and paddle. Damaged equipment not only cannot serve you well, but also makes the trip less enjoyable for others.

6) Treat all rented or borrowed equipment as if it were your own.

7) Abide by posted regulations wherever you see them.

8) Wear appropriate clothing.

9) There is no place for horseplay on a canoe trip.

10) Camp in established campsites. Where there is no option but to use a virgin camp site, leave it as near the condition you found it as possible.

Canoe Trip Equipment

For a canoe trip take only essential equipment. Fit everything in one or two waterproof duffel bags. Tie all equipment in canoe before starging each day, so it won't be lost should your canoe capsize.

Be sure not to overload your canoe. If the freeboard on your canoe when equipment and canoeists are afloat is four inches or less, you had better repack on the site and leave some of the equipment in the vehicles during the canoe trip.

A check list of equipment for a canoe trip is given on the following page. You may want to add a few items, but don't take too much.

Safety Rules for Canoe Trip

A list of twenty-five safety rules for a canoe trip is given on one of the following pages of this book. Each member of the canoe trip group must study the list and agree to observe the safety rules. Only that way can everyone enjoy a safe trip.

In addition to the safety rules given in this section of the book, you will want to review the skills taught in the section entitled "Preparing for a Safe Canoeing Experience."

Canoe Trip Equipment

GROUP:
- _____ Camera and film (may be individual instead of group)
- _____ Canoes (one per two people)
- _____ Paddles (one per person)
- _____ Extra paddles (one per canoe)
- _____ Life Jacket (one per person)
- _____ Bailing buckets
- _____ Food
- _____ Cooking equipment
- _____ Soap, towels, etc. for cooking equipment
- _____ Stove for cooking (many sites do not allow open fire)
- _____ Shelter (tents, tarps, etc.)
- _____ Extra rope (enough to portage)
- _____ Group first aid kit
- _____ Fire permit
- _____ Camp site permits
- _____ Canoe repair kit
- _____ Waterproofed bags for equipment, food, etc.
- _____ Toilet paper
- _____ Folding saw
- _____ Shovel
- _____ Game equipment (balls, etc.)
- _____ Litter bag

INDIVIDUAL:
- _____ Knee pads
- _____ Current medical exam
- _____ Drinking water (if needed)
- _____ Extra clothing
- _____ Sleeping bag
- _____ Sweater or jacket
- _____ Rainy weather gear
- _____ Sun glasses
- _____ Crash helmet (for rivers)
- _____ Hat or cap
- _____ Pocket knife
- _____ Map
- _____ Compass
- _____ Pajamas
- _____ Fishing license
- _____ Fishing equipment

_____ Swimming suit
_____ Flashlight with extra batteries & bulb
_____ Toilet paper
_____ Matches
_____ Change of shoes
_____ Eating utensils
_____ Toilet articles (soap, tooth brush, towels, etc.)
_____ Personal first aid kit with sun tan lotion, salt
tablets, insect repellent, etc.
_____ Litter bag
_____ Waterproofed bags for all equipment

Safety Rules for Canoe Trip

Many details will contribute to the safety of canoeists and equipment during a canoe trip. Here are some of the key musts:

1) Be a competent swimmer. (a must for canoeing.)

2) Wear your life jacket.

3) Never canoe alone. At least two canoes for all canoeing trips.

4) Stay close together. Lead canoe sets the pace and is never passed.

5) Lead canoe watches for hazards and directs other canoes through dangers.

6) If in doubt about the danger in any water—land—survey water from shore.

7) Don't run any rapids unless you have a guide with the group who is familiar with the river.

8) Stay off large bodies of water in wind—all water in electric storm.

9) When in doubt about any water—portage.

10) Kneel (don't sit) in the canoe.

11) Know and respect river or lake classification.

12) Respect weather conditions (even if it means a layover day)

13) Do not paddle after dark.

(continued)

14) Don't overdo the paddling—stop and rest.

15) Beware of cold water.

16) Stay close to shore whenever possible.

17) Never overload a canoe.

18) Each canoe is responsible for the canoe behind.

19) Avoid shifting your weight suddenly or leaning out.

20) If you capsize, get to the upstream end of the canoe as quickly as possible and steer the canoe toward shore. If your personal safety demands, leave the canoe and head for shore.

21) Avoid heavy or cumbersome clothing. Clothing should be light, keep you comfortable, and be easy to remove in or out of the water.

22) On a canoe trip, be sure to carry extra paddles, a first aid kit, repair kit, and flashlights.

23) Be sure you have left word of your daily destination and estimated time of return from the trip.

24) Know your canoe and your ability and stay within these limits.

25) Use common sense!

CANOE REPAIR

by Allan R. Whidden

Canoe Repair

Time and money will be saved if you understand and practice some basic canoe repair techniques. Since your canoe represents a substantial investment you will want to prolong its life expectancy. In this section we will set down some fundamental guidelines for maintaining and repairing canoes and paddles. Repairs should be few and far between. There are canoes in use today that were manufactured at the turn of the century giving good evidence that proper care and handling can preserve canoes for many years.

Aluminum

Due to the durability of aluminum, damage requiring special repairs is seldom necessary. Aluminum canoes can take a lot of abuse before serious damage is incurred. Remember though, every dent will affect, to some degree, the handling and response of the canoe. When a rip or tear in the canoe does occur there is no home remedy. A metal or machine shop can quickly and efficiently rivet an aluminum patch into place. A rubber gasket will prevent any leaks and the canoe will again be ready for use. Rivets along the seams of the canoe will work themselves loose and again the machine shop is the best place to get the canoe back in order. If you do have the necessary tools it is a relatively simple procedure to patch up the canoe. Avoid welding sections of metal or aluminum onto the canoe. The heat will weaken the aluminum surrounding the patch and will make the canoe susceptible to cracks and breaks.

For small dents a rubber mallet will help remove most of the indentations. Use a flat stable object on the opposite side of the canoe as a brace, holding it securely as the mallet strikes the protruding side. The same procedure may be used in the wilds. Soft wood covered with a coat coubles as a mallet and holding the canoe knee deep in water will serve as a makeshift brace.

Fiberglas

The strength and resilience of fiberglas has steadily improved over the last ten years. Under the proper care and handling a fiberglas canoe purchased today should seldom require repairs. Yet for the occasional accident most manufacturers of fiberglas canoes include a repair kit with the canoe. The repair kit includes easy to follow directions that do not require any extra tools. If no kit is supplied one can be obtained at a small charge from the dealer. If you are making your own repair kit it should include the following:

2-foot square piece of fiberglas

16 oz. of epoxy resin

sandpaper, medium grade

small brush applicator

Wood and Canvas

Wood and canvas canoes are slowly becoming gems of the past. More camps are transferring over to the easier to maintain aluminum and fiberglas canoes. Dry rot is the primary reason for major repairs on wood and canvas canoes. When the canoe is left sitting on damp soil bottom side up, moisture is absorbed and rot sets in. Eventually the canoe will require extensive repairs. Another problem arises when canoes are used on sandy beaches. Grains of sand become embedded in the planking creating bulges and causing wear on the canvas. The presence of sand is easily visible between the planking. A knife can be used to test wood along the gunwales, stems, and planking for the presence of rot.

Minor Repairs

White water enthusiasts are aware of the hazards involved in river running. A short tear in the canvas is a small price to pay for the thrill and exhilaration that comes when shooting rapids in an open canoe. Minor tears are frequent occurences for the avid canoeist. Some rudimentary knowledge and a little patience will put the canoe in usable shape in a few short hours.

Here are a few articles that will help make a wilderness repair an easy proceedure.

water proof cement

light canvas (No.10) one foot square

a knife

fine copper wire

materials for applying fiberglas

fiberglas

When a tear occurs, cut a portion of canvas about two inches longer than the tear and three inches wide. Allow the canoe to dry, then apply cement liberally to one side of the patch and place it under the tear with the sticky side up. If the rip is small, it may be necessary to cut the canvas at a right angle to the tear about one inch in order to get the patch underneath. Put some weight on the patch and let dry. Adding another patch over the canvas is not necessary. I've found that one patch works just as well and doesn't leave a patchwork effect on the exterior.

Major Repairs

The first step in the restoration of a canoe is to remove the gunwale and the keel by taking out the wood screws. To replace any ribs or planking necessitates peeling off the canvas. The canvas should not be used again as it will rarely return to the original shape of the canoe. Old canvas will bulge and crack much easier and shorten the life of the canoe. Once the canvas has been removed the ribs can be taken out by straightening the clinch nails on the planking and pounding them gently through. There are two types of ribs that can be purchased from the manufacturer. Some ribs are shaped to fit and others must be steam treated and bent to shape. Planking is taken off in much the same manner as the ribs. Clinch nails must be straightened and driven back out thereby loosening the planking. The manufacturer or any local lumber dealer should be able to supply you with planking the proper size. Use the old piece for size specifications. Gunwales, thwarts, and decks are also available from the manufacturer. Make certain you have the proper lengths and widths before ordering replacements.

Replacing ribs or planking involves two operations in one. A copper clinch-type or any rust proof nail is driven through the planking into the rib while a metal backing is used to clinch the nails on the inside of the rib.

This is a good time to refinish the interior of the canoe. Any commercial varnish or paint remover and a putty knife should be sufficient to remove the old finish from the ribs, planking, thwarts, and gunwales. On wood where there is excessive wear such as the gunwale, lacquer should be applied prior to the coats of marine paint or varnish.

The most involved proceedure is replacing the canvas. Once the damaged planking has been replaced, it is time to recover the canoe. Again the manufacturer is the best place to procure the canvas. A light high quality canvas is the best for a fifteen to eighteen foot canoe. Heavier canvas is more difficult to work with and the end product is a heavier craft. Applying the canvas is at least a two man job. The more helping to stretch and hold the canvas on when it is tacked down, the more secure and snug fitting it will be. There should be at least a six inch overlay of canvas on the front and on each side. The canoe should be turned upside down over a pair of sawhorses. Ideally two should stretch and another two tack down the canvas on the edge of the planking beginning at midship and working towards the ends. The canvas should be trimmed such that only enough remains to overlap the front edge. After the canvas is tacked down any bulges should be wetted. This will help shrink the canvas and make it smooth.

Canvas should be treated with a filler that is available from the manufacturer. The filler acts as a preservative on the canvas and helps to maintain a smooth, hard, protective surface. After the filler dries (usually four days to a week) apply two thin coats of varnish or marine paint. Between each coat the finish should be sanded with fine paper.

Paddles

An extra paddle per person should always be stowed with the gear on any canoe trip. Even this precaution does not preclude needed paddle repair. It is quite common for the blade of a paddle to split. There are several repair techniques. One involves the use of fine copper wire or strong fish line. Small holes are drilled or burned through the blade with a hot nail. The split blade can then be laced like a shoe and the end of the wire buried into the paddle. Another material that works well is fiberglas. A section of fiberglas can be cut to fit and applied around the blade and over the split. This adds a little weight, but will often outlast the paddle itself. Many expert canoeists apply fiberglas to the lower part of the blade for extra protection and longer life.

BIBLIOGRAPHY

Angier, Bradford and Zack Taylor. *Introduction to Canoeing*. Harrisburg, Pennsylvania: Stockpole Books, 1973.

Bearse, Ray. *The Canoe Camper's Handbook*. New York, New York: Winchester Press, 1974.

Boy Scouts of America. *Canoeing*. North Brunswick, New Jersey: Boy Scouts of America, 1974.

Boy Scouts of America. *Wilderness Voyageurs*. Region Ten, Boy Scouts of America.

Camp, Raymond Russell. *Young Sportsman's Guide to Canoeing*. New York, New York: Nelson, 1962.

Carter, Randy. *Canoeing White Water in Northern Virginia and Northeastern West Virginia also The Great Smoky Mountain Area*. Fairfax, Virginia: Louis Matacia, 1963.

Elvedt, Ruth. *Canoeing A to Z*. Minneapolis, Minnesota: Burgess Publishing Company, 1964.

Germain, Donald L. *When You Go Canoe Camping*. Nashville, Tennessee: General Board of Education of The United Methodist Church, 1968.

Handle, Carle Walker. *Canoe Camping: A Guide to Wilderness Travel*. New York, New York: The Ronald Press Company, 1953.

Handle, Carle Walker. *Canoeing*. New York, New York: A. S. Barnes and Company, 1956.

Hawksley, Oz. *Missouri Ozark Waterways*. Jefferson City, Missouri: Missouri Conservation Commission, 1965.

Leslie, Robert Franklin. *Read the Wild Water*. New York, New York: E. P. Dutton & Company, Inc., 1966.

Malo, John. *Malo's Complete Guide to Canoeing and Canoe-Camping*. Chicago, Illinois: Quadrangle Books, 1969.

Malo, John. *Wilderness Canoeing*. New York, New York: Macmillan, 1971.

McNair, Robert E. *Basic River Canoeing*. Martinsville, Indiana: American Camping Association, Inc., 1968.

New England Camping Association. *Canoeing Manual*. Somersworth, New Hampshire: Somersworth Free Press, Inc., 1952.

Perry, Ronald H. *Canoeing for Beginners*. New York, New York: Association Press, 1967.

Riviere, William A. *Pole, Paddle, & Portage*. New York, New York: Van Nostrand Reinhold Company, 1969.

Rutstrum, Calvin. *North American Canoe Country*. New York, New York: Macmillan, 1965.

Skinner, Rulon Dean. *Techniques of Outdoor Adventure*. Provo, Utah: Brigham Young University Publications, 1974.

172

The American National Red Cross. *Basic Canoeing*. Washington, D.C.: The American National Red Cross, 1965.

The Appalachian Mountain Club. *The Appalachian Mountain Club New England Canoeing Guide*. Boston, Massachusetts: The Appalachian Mountain Club, 1965.

Vaughan, Linda Kent and Richard Hale Stratton. Dubuque, Iowa: Wm. C. Brown Company Publishers, 1970.

Williams, Peter Fairney. *Canoeing Skills and Canoe Expedition Technique for Teachers and Leaders*. London, Pelham, 1967.

INDEX